Group Activities for

PERSONAL DEVELOPMENT

Group Activities for

PERSONAL DEVELOPMENT

SHEENA DUBOUST

PAMELA KNIGHT

Telford Road • Bicester
Oxon OX26 4LQ • UK

Published by
Speechmark Publishing Ltd, Telford Road, Bicester, Oxon
OX26 4LQ, United Kingdom
www.speechmark.net

© S Duboust and P Knight, 1995
Reprinted 1996, 1997, 1998, 1999, 2000, 2001, 2002

02–2548/Printed in the United Kingdom

British Library Cataloguing in Publication Data
Duboust, Sheena
   Group activities for personal development
   I. Title II. Knight, Pamela
   158.2

ISBN 0 86388 337 0
(Previously published by Winslow Press Ltd
under ISBN 0 86388 132 7)

CONTENTS

Sheena Duboust (née Duncan) has worked as Head Occupational Therapist for Mental Health Services in the Highlands in Scotland. She has a special interest in creative therapies and working with people who have been sexually abused and those with eating disorders, in group settings. Previously she worked in London in a therapeutic community and before that in general adult psychiatry.

Pamela Knight is a Senior Occupational Therapist currently working in adult general psychiatry in Scotland. She runs a programme of activities including those presented in this book. She has experience of both hospital and community work and has spent some time working as a counsellor dealing with alcohol problems and related issues.

ACKNOWLEDGMENTS

There are many people who have helped along the way with this book and we would like to take this opportunity to acknowledge them.

Thank you to: Firstly, all the patients who were willing to be 'guinea pigs' in the Communications and Assertiveness Group in the Occupational Therapy Department at Craig Dunain Hospital, Inverness, when we tried out new ideas for the workshops; Mary Campbell, the co-therapist in the group for her honest feedback and support; Jackie MacNicol for typing up the original manuscript; and finally, the other staff in the OT Department for encouraging us to go ahead with the idea of writing a book.

PREFACE

This manual has been produced for teachers, therapists and others to use with groups of people who are working on personal development issues, such as how to express feelings without fear, or how to break down problems of thinking.

We found that when we were running this type of group a lot of precious time was spent sifting through numerous books trying to compile games and exercises on a particular theme. We had also accumulated numerous exercises of our own which were recorded in a rather haphazard way.

The idea of this manual was to create a compendium of well established material from known sources, some from unknown, some which we had adapted for our own purposes and many which we had created from our own ideas and experiences. These have all gone into a series of what may be described as off the peg tried and tested sessions which should reduce otherwise lengthy preparation time for the practitioner.

WHO IS THIS MANUAL FOR?

This handbook is intended for use by people who are experienced in planning and running groups. Some of the suggested exercises employ themes and techniques that can evoke strong emotions from people participating in these sessions. It is therefore recommended that at least one leader should have a good understanding of group dynamics, be experienced in assessing members' difficulties and be skilled in planning and running activity-based groups of this kind.

We have used these activities in adult general psychiatry in a hospital setting, but we feel they have a much wider scope than this, since all of us at some time in our lives have to re-evaluate our attitudes, behaviour and coping mechanisms. In view of this we hope that the benefits of these sessions will be seen in the wider community setting, for example with youth groups, groups working on women's issues, support groups, assertion training or perhaps as part of stress management programmes or wherever people want to work together to gain better self-understanding and confidence.

HOW TO USE THIS MANUAL

Presented in a format designed for ease of use, this manual is divided into themes with several sessions on each. These sessions contain exercises which enable group participants to look at, and work on, the specific theme as well as on related issues. The appropriate session can be chosen once the group leader has identified the group and the theme on which to work.

Exercises within these sessions are interchangeable: for example you may find that a main activity working on developing self-understanding could in some instances be used to work on exploring relationships. However it is important to keep in mind the overall structure starting with an introduction and warm ups, leading into the main session and finishing with a closing exercise.

Each section begins by giving leaders a broad introduction to the themes. At the start of each session we have stated what we hope to achieve by the end of the group session. It is often useful for group leaders to highlight these aims for group members at the beginning of the group.

The timing has been worked out for groups containing 6–8 members. If numbers differ from these, the timing should be adjusted accordingly.

INTRODUCTION

There are considerable benefits to be gained from using a group setting in the pursuit of personal development. Initially a client may join the group with deep feelings of isolation, but discover that others have encountered similar problems and can share such feelings. This can bring a great sense of relief as they begin to realize that they are not alone or unique.

Having people at different stages of recovery and progress can work well since the newer members can see hope for themselves, especially if others can testify to their improvement. Often clients have a very poor opinion or image of themselves and this usually leads to feelings that they have nothing of value to offer to others. By encouraging listening and sharing we can avoid morbid preoccupations with self. The ability to give to others is valuable in the healing process and increases feelings of self-worth.

The group setting can also be seen as an educational one where, for example, in a stress management programme, symptoms of anxiety and the way these affect us physiologically and emotionally can be discussed, so helping to allay any irrational beliefs or fears. Advice from others, even if not useful, can be seen as a caring gesture. Feedback from other group members can be useful in helping develop social skills, as we learn from others how our attitudes and mannerisms are interpreted. Role-play may be used to act out specific problem areas, using other members to represent figures in our lives. This allows testing to go on in a afe environment.

Seeing how others cope with similar situations to our own may be useful and lead to experimentation with alternative coping mechanisms for ourselves. For people who find it difficult to form close relationships the group provides a safe environment to start. This is made possible by honest and open feedback from others which at the same time sustains acceptance and rapport.

In conclusion, the group is an ideal setting for discovering how we are seen by others, how our behaviour affects others and why we behave in certain ways. By gaining this understanding we can set in motion the wheels of change.

PRACTICAL CONSIDERATIONS

Qualities of a Good Group Leader

For the most effective running of each session we suggest that two group leaders are used, one of whom, as recommended earlier, should have some experience of group work. A leader showing empathy can create a safe environment for members, but they should be able to challenge members, as long as this is done in a constructive manner. Leaders also have to decide whether they will actively participate in the exercises. There are several choices:

1 Both leaders act as facilitators only and take no active part in the activities.
2 Both leaders take an active part in all exercises.
3 The leader who is introducing a particular exercise does not take an active part, while the co-leader does.

Whatever you decide, the following points should be considered: participating leaders should be aware of the other group members and offer help to any who are finding a particular exercise difficult. They should also be aware that the groups are not a forum for them to work out any personal difficulties they may have themselves. Group leaders participating can often function as role models for group members.

Open or Closed Groups?

All the sessions included in this manual have been used with open groups (those that run over a period of time and allow members to join or leave at any point) but they can of course be used with a closed group, where membership remains the same from start to finish, with the advantage of working at a deeper emotional level.

How to Select Members

Each member should be assessed individually for their suitability for the group and its functions should be explained. Clients should have identifiable difficulties in relating to others which could be worked on using group techniques. They should show a degree of willingness to work at an emotional level.

Members' Expectations

Members should be encouraged to attend a personal development group over a period of time, as attendance at one or two groups is not going to 'cure' their difficulties. The groups are a starting-point for working on issues and, as the groups last for only one hour, or just over, most of the work will happen outside these sessions. Leaders could explain that the group activities help members to gain insight, therefore enabling them to initiate change. In order for people to see and monitor changes it is a good idea for people to keep the art work, writing and so on from groups.

Frequency

We chose to run a group session once a week and found this worked well as it gave sufficient time for members to reflect and work on issues that arose from particular themes in-between times.

Room

Ensure that you have a private, closed or quiet room with minimal distraction, large enough to allow freedom of movement but not so large that people are overwhelmed by space.

Boundaries

There are many issues related to boundaries within a group that all leaders should be aware of. It is up to individual group leaders to decide on their own group rules but we have found the following to be essential in the effective running of our groups:

- Members should arrive on time; late-comers are not admitted.
- Members should be discouraged from leaving the session early.
- Members should be encouraged to join in all the exercises within a group, but if there is a particular exercise they find difficult they can sit it out and join in the next one. (Obviously, if a member is consistently opting out, this needs to be tackled.)
- Group leaders should be aware of their own boundaries: that is, they should not use the group as a stage to explore their own unresolved personal issues. Leaders should only facilitate exercises with which they themselves feel comfortable.
- Any visiting staff or new members should be told they are expected to participate; 'observers' are not allowed.
- The group should feel safe for members; group leaders should encourage members to work but not *force* them to work at a deeper emotional level than they are ready for, or is safe for them.

STRUCTURE OF GROUP SESSIONS

Each session is structured as follows:

Introduction

Warm-up(s)

Main exercise

Closure

Introduction: In an open group it is essential to begin by having members introduce themselves: even if the names will not be remembered, the process of introduction allows people to be more relaxed in approaching each other and the group will feel more cohesive.

Warm-ups act as 'ice-breakers', helping people to relax and let go of any outside business and to focus on what is going on in the group. It is unrealistic to expect members to come in 'cold' and begin to work instantly on issues of a personal nature, so it is important not to rush through these activities – good warm-ups should lead into the theme of the main exercise and therefore increase its effectiveness.

Main exercise: The overall aim is to explore the central theme of the workshop in depth. Most of the personal work is done here and that is why most time is spent on it. The exercises we have used in this book have been designed to permit every member time to explore the theme; it is therefore important that the leaders allow everyone to discuss the issues that have come up for them.

Closure: This exercise helps to bring the group back together and to summarize the work done, bringing this to a conclusion and preparing members for leaving the group. Often the exercises will encourage members to think about something they will take away with them from the group; while it is acknowledged that members will still have work to do on the related themes, the closure should help them to 'wind down'.

EXPLORING RELATIONSHIPS

Group Leader's Introduction

Making and maintaining relationships is a central and very important part of most people's lives, yet it is an area which can cause many problems and difficulties. However, we can be encouraged to identify and challenge these difficulties and to explore ways of overcoming them by dealing with them in a different way. We will be looking at the building-blocks, such as trust, expression of feelings and self-understanding, learning to listen, negotiating and caring, which go to create healthy, enjoyable relationships.

By reflecting on past relationships and our role within them we may begin to understand how they may influence present and future partnerships. Members of the groups will be encouraged to look at different types of relationships, such as those with family, friends, partners, children and colleagues. Relationships amongst group members will also be looked at to explore relevant issues.

● ACTIVITY LOCATOR

1 EXPLORING RELATIONSHIPS

AIMS
1 To identify and acknowledge personal characteristics.
2 To encourage us to think about how we are seen by others.
3 To explore what we look for and expect from friendships.
4 To gain insight into possible difficulties in becoming close to others.
5 To build up trust within the group.

MATERIALS Paper and pen for each person — at least three pieces of paper each; three extra chairs; felt-tips or crayons.

ACTIVITY	METHOD	TIME
Introduction *Qualities*	Seated in a circle, members introduce themselves and name a quality they admire in a friend.	*5 mins*
Warm-up 1 *Past meeting*	Each person is asked to think of someone from the past that they would like to meet again, and why. They then share this with the rest of the group.	*10 mins*
Warm-up 2 *Adverts*	Have each person imagine that they are putting an advert in the paper looking for a friend or partner. Each person is asked to write an advert highlighting the qualities they want in the other person and the qualities they possess themselves. Then each person reads their advert out. Discuss and expand.	*10–15 mins*
Main exercise *Three chairs*	Three chairs are set out on one side of the room, next to each other in a line. Each person is asked to sit on their own, either on a chair or on the floor. They then have to think of themselves and how other people see them and to draw their face on their first piece of paper. (This should take about 15 minutes.) Secondly they are asked to think of the person they feel closest to at this time in their life. They then draw the face of this person on their second piece of paper. Thirdly they are asked to think of someone they would like to be closer to — maybe someone they used to be close to; someone they find it difficult to be close to or someone they do not know very well yet. They then draw the face of this person on their third piece of paper.	

When everyone is finished each person in turn comes up to the three chairs. The chairs represent each of the three people drawn. Starting with the chair representing 'self', the person starts by saying a little about themselves. (While sitting in each chair they hold up the relevant drawing in front of their face.) The others are encouraged to ask questions to find out more about the person. Allow a couple of minutes for each 'chair'. After talking about themselves, the member moves on to the next chair and introduces person number 2, saying why they are close and describing that person. Similarly, with the second person, they say why they want to get closer to that person. In each case, other group members are encouraged to ask questions.

When everyone has had their turn, discussion can be facilitated by group leaders: how did members find the exercise; did they learn anything new? (This exercise can be quite powerful and can also be used as a warm-up for psychodrama or role-play.)

45 mins

Closure
Group feedback

Discussion on the previous exercise can be rounded off by asking people how they found the whole group.

5 mins

2 EXPLORING RELATIONSHIPS

AIMS

1 To explore feelings related to 'belonging' and those related to being isolated from others.
2 To identify a specific situation which we are unhappy with.
3 To identify our own needs in a relationship.
4 To promote problem solving.

MATERIALS Art paper, A4 paper, pens, paints, markers.

ACTIVITY	METHOD	TIME
Introduction *Laughter*	Members introduce themselves by saying their first name and the name of someone who makes them laugh and why.	*5 mins*
Warm-up 1 *What relationships mean to me*	Individuals are asked what is the first thing that comes to mind when they think of relationships.	*5 mins*
Warm-up 2 *Breaking down walls*	*Part 1* All of the group, apart from one, form a tight circle. The remaining person has to try and break into the circle and the group prevent this by using their bulk and cohesiveness. Members take it in turns to be the 'outsider'.	*5 mins*
	Part 2 One member of the group volunteers to stand in the middle of the circle and then tries to break out of the tight group surrounding them and, as before, the group tries to prevent this. Members again take it in turns, this time to be the 'insider'. A discussion then follows about how both situations felt for members in the various roles.	*10 mins*
Main exercise *Pictures*	Individuals are asked to draw two pictures. Picture 1 depicts a relationship they have at present but would like to change in some way; they illustrate the relationship as it is at present by using places, objects and other people that are involved in it.	*10 mins*
	Picture 2 depicts the scene as they would like it to be.	
	Ask the group to be aware of their feelings when doing each drawing.	*10 mins*
	Ask each person to talk through their scenes and share them with other members.	*20 mins*

9

Closure
Catch phrase

Ask members to think of a catch phrase that they could use that might help them make a change relating to their pictures. Some may find it useful to use pen and paper to write this initially. They are then asked to share this with others.

10 mins

3 EXPLORING RELATIONSHIPS

AIMS
1 To explore risk taking in relation to forming friendships.
2 To help identify one's own needs in a relationship.
3 To facilitate problem solving.
4 To encourage us to support one another,
   thus improving self-esteem and confidence.

MATERIALS   A4 paper and pen for each member.

ACTIVITY	METHOD	TIME
Introduction *Descriptions*	Seated in a circle, each member of the group introduces themselves and tells others what word a friend or acquaintance might use to describe them.	*5 mins*

Warm-up
Choices
	Part 1
	Members mill around the room randomly and are then told to choose a partner. The leader then asks who in the group took the initiative and chose someone, and who were the people who held back and were approached.
	    A short discussion follows on:
	(a) Is what happened a common occurrence in people's lives?
	(b) Are there risks with either role?
	
	Part 2
	Still in their pairs, members find out from their partners three qualities they would look for in a person to be a friend.
	    After this exchange each pair discloses this information to the rest of the group.
		15 mins
		
		5 mins

Main exercise *Dear Cathie*	Each person is given a piece of paper and a pen and is asked to write a letter as if to a problem page and entitle it 'Dear Cathie'. The letter should be about a relationship problem and the author will remain anonymous. When everyone has finished the letters are folded and put into a box or hat and mixed up. Each person picks out a letter and takes it in turn to read it out. The group leader facilitates a discussion on ways the problem may be eased and encourages members to share any similar experiences.	*35 mins*
Closure *What I heard*	Each person is asked to share something that they have heard that they feel might be of use to them.	*5 mins*

4 EXPLORING RELATIONSHIPS

AIMS
1 To explore the roles we take in different relationships.
2 To facilitate the feelings of being controlled and held back and, conversely, of controlling someone else.
3 To promote decision making.
4 To have a sense of fun.
5 To look at the way we work with other people.

MATERIALS See under 'Main Exercise'; glue, sellotape and scissors will also be needed.

ACTIVITY	METHOD	TIME
Introduction *Passive/active*	This introduction is done in two parts. First, each group member introduces themselves by saying their name, identifying a person in their lives with whom they take on a passive role, and saying why. Second, each member names someone with whom they take on an active or leading role, and says why.	*10 mins*
Warm-up 1 *Restrain*	The group is divided into pairs. In each pair one person stands behind the other with their arms placed securely around their partner's waist. The captive partner then has to attempt to reach the other side of the room and the restrainer has to try and prevent this. After a few minutes the pair change roles. The leader may want to raise points for discussion (eg. feelings experienced during the exercise, differences in the two roles).	*10 mins*
Warm-up 2 *Copy cat*	Members mill around the room and any one person starts the game by initiating an action which the others then have to imitate. This action is repeated until another member changes it. This action is then imitated and so it continues. Vocals may be added for interest if you wish.	*5 mins*
Main exercise *The task*	The main group is divided up into smaller teams of 3 or 4 members. Each team is given an identical collection of materials. They are then given the task of assembling them into whatever form they wish. Each team is given the same amount of time for this purpose. Materials might include: paper, card, foil, fabric, pipe-cleaners, straws, cotton, feathers, wool and so on. Glue, scissors and sellotape will also be needed.	

The main group then reassembles, displaying their creations. This is followed by a discussion about the roles that were adopted by each member in the team. Who emerged as leader? How were decisions made? Did anyone work on their own? How did it feel to be in a particular role, and is this the role which was normally adopted in other areas of life?

30–40 mins

Closure
Relaxation with unguided visualization

The leader arranges the group in the relaxation position suggested on page 107 and uses the following text.

'First make yourself completely comfortable. If you are wearing glasses take them off and loosen any tight clothing at your neck and waist. Allow your body to sink into the floor. Let your legs and feet flop outwards. Enjoy the feeling of resting, of being completely supported. Let your eyes close.'

Pause...
'Now become aware of your breathing. Follow the breath as it comes into and goes out of your body. Do not try to control it in any way – just observe the natural rhythm of your breathing. As you breathe out, imagine your whole body growing limp and heavy. Each time you breathe out, imagine that you are letting tension flow out of your body and mind. Focus on the word 'peace' as the breath flows gently in and out of your body.'

Pause...
'Now that your body is relaxed, let yourself drift in your imagination to a place of great beauty and peace. This might be somewhere you know well in real life, or it might be completely imaginary. Become aware of the harmony and tranquillity of your surroundings. You feel perfectly calm and at peace in this place. Become aware of the position of your body; notice what you are touching with the different parts of your body. Become aware of the objects nearest to you – how close are they? Can you reach out and touch them? What are their shapes, textures, colours and smells? Can you hear anything? What kind of sound is it? Is it nearby or in the distance? Is there any movement in your scene, or is everything completely still?'

'Now take your attention away from your immediate surroundings and look into the distance. What can you see as your gaze travels as far as the eye can see? Is anything happening in this wider scene? Can you describe it to yourself?'

Pause...
'Become aware of things which are closest to you. Again notice their colours, shapes, size, smells. Because you feel relaxed and calm, all your senses are unusually alert and you feel, see, taste and smell things more vividly than in everyday life. Enjoy this feeling of being completely alive and responsive to your surroundings. Enjoy the freedom to do anything you like – to stay inside your special place and explore it more fully, or to move on to another place altogether.'

Long pause...
'Shortly I am going to bring this session to an end, so, in your own time, begin to move slowly away from your scene. Become aware of the feelings of peace and tranquillity which you are bringing back with you.'

   'When you are ready, have a good stretch and slowly bring yourself back into the room. Take your time before getting up, and when you sit up, remember to do so slowly.'

10 mins

5 EXPLORING RELATIONSHIPS

AIMS
1 To highlight how our behaviour affects others.
2 To explore the dynamics in some of our relationships.
3 To show how others view us.

MATERIALS A4 paper, art paper, markers, pens/pencils.

ACTIVITY	METHOD	TIME
Introduction *Close descriptions*	Members introduce themselves and, in a few words, say how the closest person to them might describe them to others.	*5 mins*
Warm-up 1 *Bad habits*	Individuals are asked to think of a characteristic/habit they have that they feel upsets others.	*5 mins*
Warm-up 2 *First impressions*	Members mill around the room and when the leader shouts 'stop', they turn to the person nearest to them and tell them what their first impression of them was. Repeat several times.	*10 mins*
Main exercise *Lines*	Participants are asked to depict certain relationships in their lives in diagram form. The leader may wish to draw the example on page 18 to demonstrate. The quality of the relationship can be highlighted by the various symbols. The group then reassembles and is invited to talk through the diagrams and share them with others.	*15 mins for diagrams, 20 mins for discussion*
Closure *Private note*	Members are asked to write a private note or letter to a person who came up in one of the relationships and to take this away with them when they leave.	*5 mins*

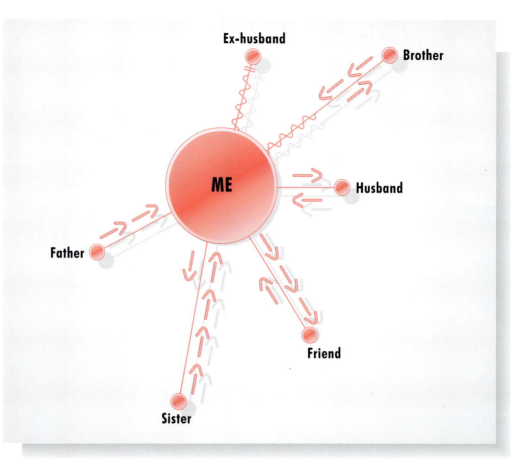

 Zigzag lines show stress in a relationship (eg. brother, ex-husband).

Two straight lines shows relationship has ended (eg. ex-husband).

 Arrows pointing towards the centre show energy flow coming from others to you (eg. father).

 Arrows pointing outwards from the centre show energy flow coming from you to others (eg. sister, husband, friend).

 The number of arrows shows the balance of energy flow eg. there is equal input between the central figure and husband, but variabilities with others.

LEARNING TO TRUST

②

Group Leader's Introduction

In order to have fulfilling, close relationships we need to learn to trust each other. We have a basic instinct to protect ourselves and in some instances it is important that we retain this instinct at a certain level. However we have to be careful not to isolate ourselves in an attempt to remain safe. Finding people we can trust carries a degree of risk: some will respect our trust and be worthy of it, some may not.

Sharing with others can be a rewarding experience, aiding relaxation and reducing feelings of isolation and loneliness. Learning to trust can allow us to 'be ourselves' and be accepted for what we are which in turn helps build confidence and self-esteem. It should help us to accept others, too.

Many of the exercises within the workshop enable us to test out trust within a safe environment.

● ACTIVITY LOCATOR

1 LEARNING TO TRUST

AIMS
1 To facilitate trust within the group.
2 To experience touching and being touched by others.
3 To develop an understanding of trust.

MATERIALS None.

Note: The members of this group should know each other reasonably well.

ACTIVITY	METHOD	TIME
Introduction *Someone I can trust*	Each member says their own name, then the name of one person in their life they feel they can trust, and why.	*5 mins*
Warm-up 1 *Personal space*	The leader asks each member to choose a partner; one person stands at one end of the room, the other opposite them at the other end of the room. They then walk towards each other and stop at whatever distance feels comfortable for them. This is then discussed, with aspects such as distance, closeness, eye contact and touch being highlighted (A variation can be to repeat this exercise – first with partners who do not know each other and then with partners who do – and see if there are any differences in the distance between them when they need to stop.)	*10 mins*
Warm-up 2 *Palm reading*	Staying with the same partner, members are asked, taking it in turns, to 'read' their partner's palm. To do this they tell their partner anything that they have discovered about them by looking at and touching their hand: for example, are they married (wearing a wedding ring); do they bite their nails; do they smoke? Again, at the end of this activity, discussion is encouraged. How did people find the exercise and what did they learn about their partner?	*10 mins*
Main exercise *Desert island*	In this exercise everyone is asked to stand up and move all the furniture, so that there is space to move around. The leader asks members to touch the shoulder of someone they would choose for the following situations, giving their reasons for each choice: (a) to be on a desert island with; (b) to hold the end of a rope for them when they are climbing;	

(c) to go shopping with;

(d) to cook a meal for;

(e) to nurse them when they are ill;

(f) to go on a night out with;

(g) to go on holiday with;

(h) to trust with a secret.

25 mins

Closure
Bridges

Several members of the group arrange themselves side by side on their hands and knees so that they form a sort of bridge. A volunteer carefully lies face-up on top of their backs. The 'Bridge' sways gently from side to side and backwards and forwards. Members change positions regularly so that all members have participated.

10 mins

2 LEARNING TO TRUST

AIMS
1 To explore issues related to trust.
2 To identify how we feel about trusting others.
3 To facilitate change where appropriate.

MATERIALS   Paper and pen for each member.

ACTIVITY	METHOD	TIME
Introduction *TV personalities*	Each member says their name and tells the group a television personality they would not trust, and why.	*5 mins*
Warm-up 1 *Assumptions*	Have people think about assumptions they often make about the trustworthiness of a person because of, say, their mannerisms, physical appearance, religious beliefs and so on. Ask each person in turn to name one such assumption.	*10 mins*
Warm-up 2 *Wobbly knees*	Everyone stands in a circle, or in a file, one behind the other, and then tries to sit on the knees of the person behind them without falling down. This exercise may need several attempts.	*10 mins*
Main exercise *Swimming pool*	Tell members that they are to imagine the room is a swimming pool. Designate areas of the room to represent the shallow, middle and deep ends, the bar, diving-board and lounging-about area. Ask members to place themselves in the area that relates to the way they feel about trusting people. Once everyone has done that, ask them to say how they feel in a few words in their chosen position. Then ask members, if they could choose another position, what it would be. Have them move to the chosen area to see how it feels. Once this exercise has been completed, leaders can facilitate discussion on the information that has become available from members during the group. The focus should be on any changes they would like to make and why.	*20–25 mins*
Closure *Private writing*	Ask members to write down privately the name of someone they would like to trust more. They take this away with them, without disclosing the information.	*5 mins*

3 LEARNING TO TRUST

AIMS
1 To encourage discussion of trust.
2 To generate feelings about trusting.
3 To promote touching between members.

MATERIALS   A4 paper and pens for each member, several scarves.

ACTIVITY	METHOD	TIME
Introduction *Trust me*	Each member introduces themselves and tells the group something they could do to show that they could be trusted.	*5 mins*
Warm-up 1 *Blind walk*	This is a well known exercise. Members are asked to choose a partner; one person is blindfolded. Their partner has to lead them around the room, using as much physical contact as both feel comfortable with, such as holding one hand, supporting an elbow and forearm, arm around waist, and introduce them to different objects, textures and people. After 2 or 3 minutes, they change places. The leader facilitates discussion on the following questions: (a) Which role did you prefer? (b) How did each role feel?	*10–15 mins*
Warm-up 2 *Touch and tell*	If the main group is large, divide it into smaller groups of four or five. One member volunteers to go into the middle of the room and to be blindfolded. Other members then come forward and the 'blind' person touches their clothes and tries to identify the individuals. The first person correctly identified then becomes the 'blind' one. The warm-up can then progress to just touching hands and then to touching faces. Discuss afterwards how members found the exercise.	*10–15 mins*
Main exercise *Who to trust*	Ask members to get into pairs and discuss what makes us trust some people and not others. It may be useful to use pen and paper for this activity. Allow 10 minutes for this and then ask members to come back into the large group and expand on the discussion.	*25–30 mins*
Closure *Showing trust*	Ask each member to go up to somebody and show them physically that they can trust them. If they feel the need they can show them verbally too.	*5 mins*

4 LEARNING TO TRUST

AIMS
1 To promote trust through touching.
2 To explore issues related to feeling safe.
3 To experience a feeling of safety.

MATERIALS Pillows and relaxation mats.

ACTIVITY	METHOD	TIME
Introduction *A safe place*	Members are seated on chairs in a circle. The leader asks each person to introduce themselves and to tell the others, briefly, about a place where they feel safe.	*5 mins*
Warm-up *Biodynamic lifting*	Ask members to get into pairs, one to be A, the other to be B. Ask A to lie on the floor on their back. B kneels behind A's head, facing them. Explain that the exercise involves B lifting parts of A's body to discover areas of tension and areas of relaxation. It may be helpful for two leaders to demonstrate this exercise, which should be gentle and slow. B should start by lifting A's head slightly off the floor, supporting it firmly with the palms of the hand. The head should be lifted up and down *carefully*, encouraging A to let B take all the weight of the head. The head can also be moved gently from side to side. B should be aware of any resistance from A and can feed this back to them. Similarly A can let B know if they are being too quick or too firm in their handling. Once B has finished lifting the head they should move round to one side of A and do the same to the arm, followed by the leg, other leg and then the other arm. Again this should be taken slowly and gently and B should be aware of any tensions. When they have finished, repeat the exercise, with A doing the lifting and B lying on the floor. There should be feedback between pairs as to how they find this exercise.	*10 mins*
Main exercise *Group sculpt*	Ask each member to close their eyes and visualize their place of safety in detail. To help the process, offer prompts; for example: 'Be aware of what you can see – is it outside or inside? What noises can you hear? Are there any smells? What can you feel? Are there different textures? What is it that makes you feel safe here?	

Are there any other people here or are you here on your own? Are there any pets or animals?'

Then ask members to open their eyes and find out if anyone would like to create their place of safety in the group. This will be done by using the room and the other people to represent important objects, people and so on in their scene. Ask the volunteer to describe their place as they walk about the room and to choose what and who they want in their scene, giving the reasons for their choice and saying what makes their place feel safe.

Let the person relax into their scene for several minutes when they have completed it.

This exercise can be repeated by as many people as want to do it and as there is time for. Discuss participants' feelings arising from the exercise.

40 mins

Closure
Biodynamic lifting

Repeat the warm-up in the same pairs and ask members to notice any differences.

10 mins

5 LEARNING TO TRUST

AIMS
1. To inform members of the benefits of relaxation.
2. To practise simple massage techniques.
3. To promote trust.
4. To create a feeling of relaxation.

MATERIALS Towels, massage oil, essential oils to promote relaxation: for example, camomile and lavender (beware of any contraindications).

Note: Preferably group members should have worked together previously.

ACTIVITY	METHOD	TIME
Introduction Aids to relaxation	Members are seated on chairs in a circle. They introduce themselves in turn and tell others some things which help them to relax.	*5 mins*
Warm-up What is massage?	The leader ascertains from members whether they have had a massage before, what their understanding of it is and their feelings about it. The leader then informs members about the benefits of massage, using information on the handout (pages 31–33).	*10–15 mins*
Main exercise Simple massage	The leader explains that members are now invited to experience giving and receiving simple forehead, shoulder and neck massage. There are suggestions on the attached handout for those who have great difficulty with being touched by others and would rather massage themselves. Members form pairs; the receiver sits on a chair and the masseur stands behind. Each pair can take a towel, some massage oil and essential oils if they wish. It is not necessary to use oils. The leader directs the massage as described in the handout, using either another leader or group members to demonstrate.	*30–40 mins*
Closure Massage feedback	In a large group the leader encourages members to discuss feelings experienced during the exercise and asks them to say whether they would choose to have a massage again or not, giving their reasons.	*5 mins*

MASSAGE

OF FOREHEAD, SHOULDERS AND NECK

Massage has many values and everyone can impart and receive its effects. It can:

- reduce tension in the muscles;
- reduce pain;
- stimulate circulation;
- help eliminate waste products from muscle cells;
- reduce emotional tension and anxiety;
- help to promote a feeling of relaxation and well-being.

It is therefore an important element in stress management and can be used to promote trust.

Before giving a massage there are some important guidelines to follow:

- Make sure the room is warm and that the masseur's hands are warm also, as muscles cannot relax when cold.
- The masseur's nails should be short. All jewellery which is likely to catch on skin, hair or clothes should be removed.
- The masseur should place their hands on their partner for a few moments, holding them still. The masseur breathes calmly and slowly so that they can feel relaxed.
- Both masseur and partner should be in positions which are comfortable and promote relaxation.

HOW TO GIVE A MASSAGE

- During the massage, always keep one hand in contact with the skin; this promotes continuity.
- Use firm, deliberate and rhythmical strokes. Always check with your partner that the degree of pressure is right.
- Massage should not hurt.
- When nearing the end of the massage, indicate this by using a few slower, more deliberate strokes.
- As at beginning, when the massage is complete, keep your hands, still, on your partner for a few minutes.

TECHNIQUES

Forehead

A group member sits in a chair. The masseur stands behind, close enough to allow the other person's head to rest against their body.

1 Place both hands on the forehead, with fingertips lightly touching. The hands are moved out towards the temples, and then either into the hairline in a sweeping upwards movement or towards the cheekbones in a downward movement, finishing at the level of the ear.

2 Using hands alternately, smooth up over the forehead from the bridge of the nose to the hairline. As one hand reaches the top, begin smoothing upwards with the other, so that one hand is always in contact with the head.

Shoulders and neck

Positions are as for forehead massage.

1 Hands are cupped round the sides of the neck, just below the ears. Hands are then moved down the neck, over the tops of the shoulder, and off the ends of the shoulders in a sweeping movement, as if 'brushing away' tension. Repeat this several times.

2 Hands are placed on the tops of shoulders with fingers facing forwards and thumbs downwards. Using the rest of the hand to counterbalance the pressure, make small circling movements with the thumbs, outwards from the area near the spine, over all the upper back area. Do not massage over the spine itself. Use the fleshy part of the thumb and not the tip.

Self-massage

There may be people in your groups who do not want to be touched or who find massage threatening. For them self-massage can help. They should be encouraged to try out the techniques on themselves – massaging of our forehead and temples is something we often do naturally if we have a headache.

DEVELOPING SELF-UNDERSTANDING

Group Leader's Introduction

Why is insight important? It can help identify situations in our lives which we may find difficult. By gaining some understanding of ourselves we can begin to see what types of behaviour can irritate us or attract us to other people. We can identify in ourselves weaknesses and strengths of character and then choose to take steps to improve or draw on them, or just accept the way we are.

Honest feedback from others can help us realize how our attitudes and behaviour are interpreted and how they affect the people around us. By knowing ourselves better we can begin to predict how we may react in particular situations. Insight in itself does not necessarily bring change, but it does provide us with a basis for change if we want to take up the challenge.

The groups work on the premise that we are willing to explore issues concerning our characters and life styles.

3

● ACTIVITY LOCATOR

1 DEVELOPING SELF-UNDERSTANDING

AIMS
1 To encourage commitment and a sense of responsibility within the group.
2 To develop a sense of trust.
3 To encourage self-disclosure.

MATERIALS None.

ACTIVITY	METHOD	TIME
Introduction *Help or sabotage*	With the group seated, the leader asks each member (1) to introduce themselves; (2) to complete the following sentences: (a) 'I can help this group by . . .' (For example, listening to others/being open and honest.); (b) 'I can sabotage this group by . . .' (For example, interrupting others/being dishonest.)	*10 mins*
Warm-up 1 *Nicknames*	Ask the group to divide up into pairs and to take a couple of minutes each to tell their partners about a nickname or pet name they were once given, by whom, and how they felt about it. If any have difficulties with this they may instead want to say who they were named after and why, and how that feels. The pairs then form a main group again and members recall what their partners told them and disclose this to the others.	*10–15 mins*
Warm-up 2 *Sculptures*	Have members arrange themselves in the same pairs and take it in turns to sculpt each other into a pose which they feel depicts part of their partner's personality. Each holds their pose (where comfort allows) and the sculptor explains why they have modelled them in this fashion. The person being sculpted should be invited to comment on the accuracy of this.	*10–15 mins*
Main exercise *Cogwheel*	With the group standing, the leader arranges them into two concentric circles, with the same number of people in each. The inner circle faces outwards, the outer inwards, so that participants face each other. The leader starts by asking the group to disclose to the person they are facing: (a) two things they like about themselves. When this has been done the members of the outer circle move in a clockwise direction to face the next person. The leader then asks the group to: (b) disclose two things they dislike about themselves;	

(c) something they would like to change about themselves;

(d) something they would like to change about the other person;

(e) a fear they have;

(f) something they feel strongly about;

(g) something they are good at;

(h) something other people say they're good at.

After each statement the outer circle moves on one place, so that by the end of the exercise everyone has revealed some things about themselves to most of the members of the group.

25 mins

Closure
Something I learned today

With the group seated again in a circle, the leader asks each member in turn to think of something they learned about themselves from the exercises.

5 mins

Recommendations
This workshop will work better if most of the participants have a degree of familiarity, in view of Warm-up 2. However, if the sculpting poses a problem, the members can always sculpt on first impressions, which can also provide valuable feedback for each partner.

2 DEVELOPING SELF-UNDERSTANDING

AIMS
1. To have some fun.
2. To heighten awareness of our behaviour and how that affects relationships.
3. To help identify some personal needs.

MATERIALS Paints, crayons, water, paint brushes, art paper, various objects of interest.

ACTIVITY	METHOD	TIME
Introduction *Metaphor game*	Seated in a circle, each member introduces themselves and completes the following sentence: 'If I were an article of clothing I would be a . . .' Leaders may wish to change the metaphor to suit the group; other topics might be: type of holiday, tree, drink and so on.	*10 mins*
Warm-up 1 *Change the object*	The leader brings in several objects of interest and one is passed around the group. Each member has to improvise and mime what the object could become. Other objects can be introduced at various stages.	*10 mins*
Warm-up 2 *Personal facts*	Members mill around the room and as they pass another person they share a fact about themselves, such as 'I am allergic to fish' or 'I love holidays abroad'.	*5 mins*
Main exercise *The jungle*	Roll out a large sheet of art paper or make one by sticking several smaller pieces together. Have a variety of art materials and ask members to choose their medium. Have participants imagine themselves as a particular animal, to think what sort of habitat they would have, consider if any other animals of their type would be there with them, then illustrate this on a section of the art paper. Allow 15 minutes for this. Hand out paper and pens to all group members. Ask them to look at the illustrations near their own and create a short story involving the other animals around them. Then invite them to share their story with others. Questions for the leader to raise might include: (a) Are the animals hidden, protected, exposed or camouflaged?	

(b) Are they with others of their kind or are they solitary?

(c) What characteristics does the animal have? Are they, for example, shy, ferocious or vulnerable? Do any of these reflect how people are in reality?

30mins

Closure
Animal traits

What quality did members like most about their animal, and why?

5 mins

3 DEVELOPING SELF-UNDERSTANDING

AIMS
1 To highlight strengths of character.
2 To encourage honest feedback between group members.
3 To promote a sense of identity.

MATERIALS Art paper, selection of art media, buttons.

ACTIVITY	METHOD	TIME
Introduction *A country of interest*	Seated in a circle, group members state their names and say what country they would like to visit, and why.	5 mins
Warm-up 1 *Opposites*	People mill around the room and as they pass others they tell them something about themselves that is either the opposite of what they are or is otherwise untrue.	5 mins
Warm-up 2 *My three strengths*	Individuals are to imagine that they are going to work in or visit an underdeveloped country and to think of three personality traits they possess which they could draw on during their time there; they then share this with the other members.	10 mins
Main exercise *Noah's Ark*	Briefly the leader ensures that everyone knows the story of Noah's Ark. (See page 43.) Members are asked to draw their own Ark and to consider what would be the important things in their lives that they would take with them in it, remembering that what is left can never be retrieved. They can draw these people or items, write them down or can use buttons to represent them. When they have finished, members are invited to go through their illustration and share it with others.	30–35 mins
Closure *Something I learned today*	The leader asks each member to say something they have learned about themselves during the session.	5–10 mins

Recommendation
In the main exercise, participants may opt for items such as washing machines or vacuum cleaners, working on a fairly superficial level. If leaders want to avoid this they may wish to give some examples to show the level of participation expected.

THE STORY OF NOAH'S ARK

This story is written in the Old Testament in the Bible. Briefly what happens is that Noah is told by God that there is going to be a flood which will cover the whole world and destroy everything. He is told that he can take his family and one of each sex of all the animals he can find and to build an Ark to accommodate them all. When Noah has done this, with all his family and animals on board, it rains for 40 days and nights. Everything outside of the Ark is destroyed.

4 DEVELOPING SELF-UNDERSTANDING

AIMS
1 To help identify personal needs.
2 To encourage honest feedback from group members.
3 To highlight the point that stress means different things to different people and to show how it can affect our behaviour.

MATERIALS
Large-sized paper, overhead projector, pens, felt-tipped markers, *Blu-Tack* or drawing pins.

ACTIVITY	METHOD	TIME
Introduction *Desert island*	Each member is asked to introduce themselves, then name three survival aids they would choose to take on a desert island with them. Next they are asked to name three things of sentimental value they would also choose to take	5 mins
Warm-up *Causes and effects of stress*	Ask members to get into pairs and find a space in the room. Each person is to find out, firstly, what makes their partner feel stressed and, secondly, what they do in response to this. Then members are asked to come back to form the large group and to introduce their partner, summarizing causes of their stress and their responses to it.	15 mins
Main exercise *Silhouettes*	Again in pairs, members are asked to draw their partner's profile by using the overhead projector and a large piece of paper pinned on the wall. The leader ensures that all these are named. Everyone's profile is stuck up on the wall or spread on the floor, depending on availability of space. Members are then asked to write comments on others' profiles regarding their personality, habits and so on, being as honest as possible. When everyone has finished, each member takes it in turn to run through comments written on their profile and is encouraged to ask individuals to clarify anything they are unsure of. The leader facilitates discussion on how people felt about what was written about them.	30–35 mins
Closure *Something I learned today*	Each member is invited to tell the group something they have learned about themselves and to choose one comment that has particularly appealed to them.	5 mins

5 DEVELOPING SELF-UNDERSTANDING

AIMS
1 To help establish a sense of identity.
2 To encourage feedback between group members.
3 To encourage self-disclosure.

MATERIALS Art paper, coloured markers or pencils.

ACTIVITY	METHOD	TIME
Introduction *Think of a name*	Members introduce themselves and say whether they like their name and, if they could change it, what name they would choose, and why.	*5 mins*
Warm-up *Zoo*	The leader hands out a piece of paper to each person and has them tear it up into as many pieces as there are people in the group. They then write down the names of each person on the pieces (one name for each piece of paper). The leader asks what animal each person makes them think of, and to write it down against their name. When they are finished each member in turn reads out their list, giving the reason for their choice of animal.	*15 mins*
Main exercise *Tree of life*	Members are asked to draw a tree with roots and branches. The tree will be used as a symbol to represent influences in people's lives; for example, roots represent people and places influencing their early development and the branches represent influences which are important in their lives now. The leader may wish to draw up the example given below as a guide. Members are then invited to describe their particular tree.	*40 mins*
Closure *New growth*	Individuals think of a new shoot or branch they would like to see in the future and share this thought with the rest of the group.	*10–15 mins*

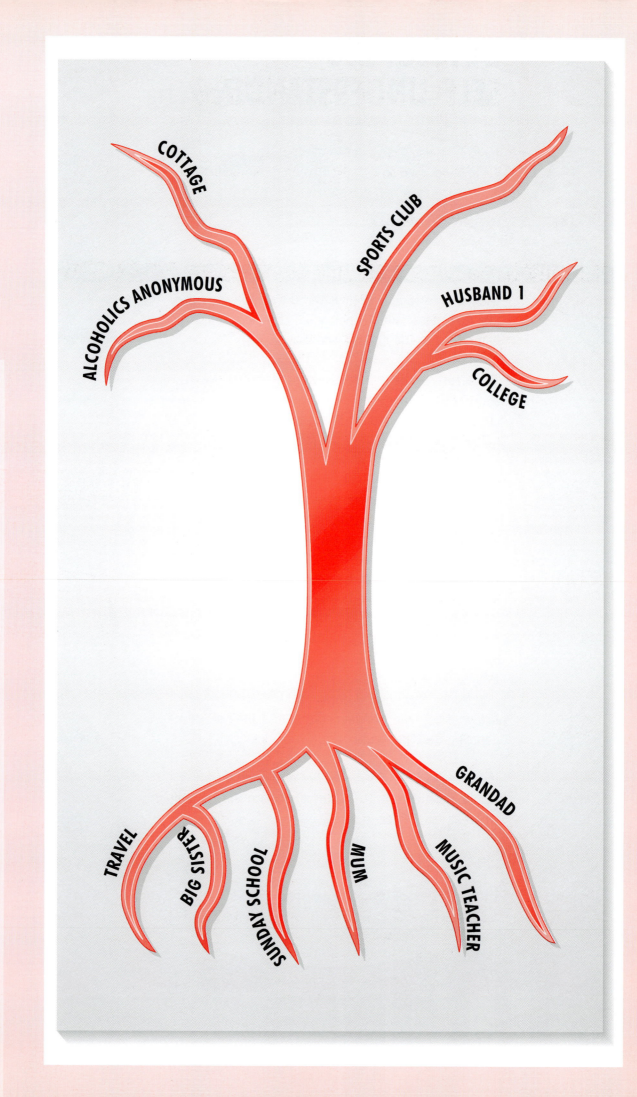

6 DEVELOPING SELF-UNDERSTANDING

AIMS
1 To help establish a sense of identity.
2 To help acknowledge personality traits.
3 To have fun.

MATERIALS   Pens and writing paper.

ACTIVITY	METHOD	TIME
Introduction *Name origins*	Seated in a circle, group members take turns to introduce themselves and describe how they come to be so named: perhaps they were named after a family friend or a family member. Do they feel they have inherited any of the characteristics of that person, along with the name?	*5–10 mins*
Warm-up 1 *Scotch broth*	Remaining seated, each member chooses an ingredient of Scotch broth, such as lentils, barley, peas, carrot, turnip, onions, leeks, mutton, salt, water, or stock. One of the chairs is removed. A volunteer then stands in the middle of the group and shouts out two or more of the ingredients that were chosen. These people then have to change their seats while the person in the middle tries to beat one of them to it. Whoever is left without a seat stands in the middle and the process begins again. At any time the middle person can shout out 'Scotch broth!', which means that everyone in the group has to change seats.	*5 mins*
Warm-up 2 *Similarities and differences*	Each member is asked to choose a partner with whom to sit somewhere in the room. They then have a short chat to discover three things they have in common and three things that are quite different about them. If necessary, these can be written down. When everyone has done this they then form the large group again and share what they have discovered.	*15 mins*
Main exercise *Sociogrammes*	The group leader explains that there is an imaginary line from one end of the room to the other; there is a scale along it with extremes of a particular personality trait at each end. For example: passive – aggressive impulsive – thoughtful relaxed – tense	

towards their identified goals. This statement should be a realistic one. When statements are completed, individuals enclose them in the envelopes provided, add their name and address and seal them. The leader collects the envelopes and posts them at an agreed time, say, 2 months later.

10 mins

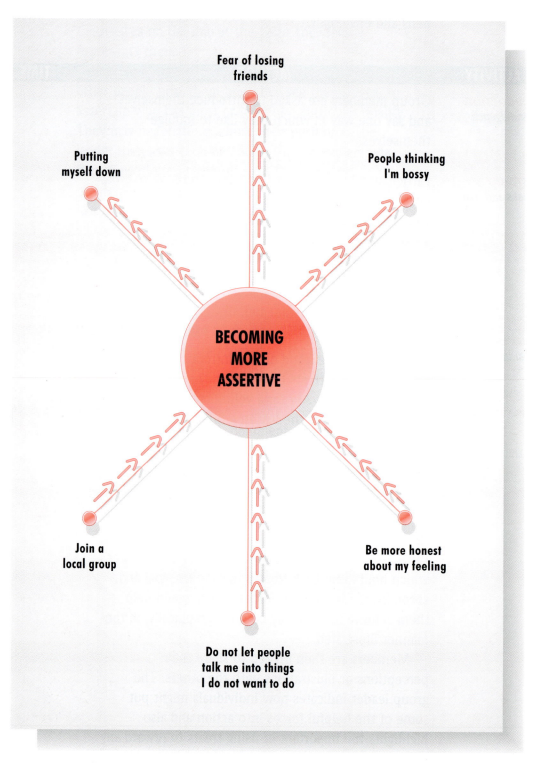

The goal is the area in the centre.

 The arrows moving away from the goal are forces that hold us back.

The arrows moving towards the goal are forces that can help us achieve it.

NON-VERBAL COMMUNICATION

Group Leader's Introduction

Non-verbal communication, or 'Body Language' as it is often referred to, is the most primitive form of communication and, unlike speech, it crosses cultural and class boundaries.

We often use words as a smokescreen to cover true feelings, but it is more difficult to hide feelings revealed by our gestures and expressions. By learning about body language we can go some way to understanding what others may be feeling, which, it is hoped, may lead to more rewarding experiences. Feedback from the group helps us to see messages that we give out to others, by our own expressions and gestures for example.

Some of the exercises in this section promote touching, which is an important part of learning to communicate on an emotional level. A touch of the hand can often be more reassuring than any well chosen words. Some people, especially those who rely on the power of speech, may find touching difficult, but they should persevere, because generally this is a rewarding practice for both giver and receiver.

④

● ACTIVITY LOCATOR

1 NON-VERBAL COMMUNICATION

AIMS
1 To encourage awareness of non-verbal communication.
2 To promote insight into the way others see us.
3 To facilitate expression of feelings using non-verbal methods.

MATERIALS Small cards with different emotions written on them.

ACTIVITY	METHOD	TIME
Introduction *Name Game*	Members are asked by the group leader to say their own name, plus a Native American name with the action to describe it: for example, 'Running Water' or 'Swift Arrow'.	5 mins
Warm-up 1 *Toe to top*	The group are asked to mill around the room, initially looking at the floor, then moving to foot level, then knees, then waists, shoulders and finally to the eyes. This should be done *gradually*. Discuss the experience afterwards. What was most difficult? What was the easiest, and why?	10 mins
Warm-up 2 *Mime the proverb*	The leader prepares some cards, enough for the number in the group. Each card has a different proverb or saying written on it. Suggested list: Let sleeping dogs lie. A bird in the hand is worth two in the bush. It's no use crying over spilt milk. Still waters run deep. Every cloud has a silver lining. He who laughs last laughs longest. The early bird catches the worm. While the cat is away the mice will play. Absence makes the heart grow fonder. United we stand, divided we fall. The leader places the cards in the middle of the floor; each member in turn collects a card and mimes the proverb for the rest to guess. They may use props around the room if they like, or other members to help, remembering they can only instruct them non-verbally.	15 mins
Main exercise *Sculpting*	Group members pair off; one partner becomes the sculptor and the other a piece of clay. The sculptor then moulds the clay into a pose which they feel	

4

depicts the partner's personality. Discussion from other group members should be encouraged. The person in the pose should be asked to comment on the accuracy of this.

20–25 mins

Closure
Gifts

Members are asked to form the main group again and take it in turns to mime a gift to offer the person on their left.

5–10 mins

2 NON-VERBAL COMMUNICATION

AIMS
1 To give and receive feedback from others.
2 To become aware of what we are projecting by our non-verbal language.
3 To encourage members to learn how to support each other.

MATERIALS   Video camera and video recorder. Prepared cards with role-play situations.

ACTIVITY	METHOD	TIME
Introduction *Names and actions*	Members standing in a circle introduce themselves and perform an action (clap their hands, take a bow, stand on one leg, and so on). All together the others in the group repeat the name and the action. (Another round can be added to this, following the same procedure, but this time with the name and action followed by a sound.)	*5 mins*
Warm-up *I see, I feel, I imagine*	Seated in a circle, the group members are asked to turn their attention to the person on their left. They are then asked: (a) to describe what they see to the rest of the group: colour of hair, dress, posture and so on; (b) to describe the feelings they have about this person: for example, I feel they are sad, I feel they are angry, I feel they are lonely; (c) to say what, from their observations and feelings, they imagine about the person: for example, I imagine that Ann would be a good sportswoman. The leader invites members to comment on the accuracy of the description.	*15 mins*
Main exercise *What's the problem?*	The leader issues cards on which a selection of situations have been written out that evoke feelings such as anger, pride, love, frustration and disbelief (see suggestions on page 59). Members are asked to find themselves a partner and one chooses to act out the situation, improvising as they go, while the other agrees to listen. The person talking is allowed a few minutes to think themselves into the role. During the role-play the leader videos each pair, focusing on facial expressions and gestures.	

The video is then played back *without sound* for all to view and members have to try and work out what feelings are being shown by expression and gesture.

The leader initiates discussion on the following:

(a) What enables us to guess what was being said?

(b) Is speech an effective smokescreen in hiding what we really feel?

(c) Do we often ignore non-verbal cues and rely too much on the spoken word?

35–40 mins

Closure
Goodbye

Members move around the room and say goodbye to everyone without using speech, trying to use a different gesture for each person: shaking hands, a hug, a pat on the back, a wave, a smile and so on.

5 mins

NON-VERBAL COMMUNICATION

1 You have just discovered you are pregnant. You are single and have just started a course at college. You are not sure how your boyfriend will react or what course of action to take.

2 Your boss has called you for a meeting with the doctor from Occupational Health because she thinks that your sick record has been poor recently. You feel this is unwarranted and are angry, but also fearful that you might be sacked.

3 Your son/daughter/mother/father has come first in a national competition. You feel proud and are full of admiration. You feel they deserved it.

4 You have just discovered that you have won a large amount of money. You feel happy but also a bit overwhelmed. You still cannot believe it.

3 NON-VERBAL COMMUNICATION

AIMS
1 To promote discussion on what components are involved in non-verbal communication.
2 To have fun.
3 To promote insight into oneself.

MATERIALS Flip-chart and markers, A4 paper and pens.

ACTIVITY	METHOD	TIME
Introduction *Greetings*	Each member is asked to introduce themselves by saying their first name. Then, milling round the room, without talking, they greet each person they pass in the following ways, at the leader's command: smiling, winking, waving, shaking hands, patting on the shoulder.	*5 mins*
Warm-up 1 *Feelings*	Each person is asked to turn to the person on their left and to say how they think they are feeling.	*5 mins*
Warm-up 2 *What is non-verbal communication?*	The leader asks for a volunteer from the group to write on the flip-chart. Participants are then asked to 'brainstorm' what is meant by 'non-verbal communication'. For example: how did they arrive at the description of their neighbour's feelings in the previous exercise? Leaders ensure that the following areas are discussed: eye contact, posture, facial expression, personal space, touch, movement, gesture.	*15 mins*
Main exercise *Doubling*	Each member is asked to choose a partner and find a space in the room. The couple then take it in turns to talk about themselves for two or three minutes each. The conversation should be quite broad, covering, for example, place of birth, school, family, work, hobbies and so on. Members are asked to pay attention, not only to what their partner is saying, but also to the way they are saying it. Issue pen and paper to participants if they would find it useful to jot down observations. The pairs then come back to form the main group and are asked to introduce their partners by 'becoming' them and relating what was actually said, but also by saying what they feel was implied by the non-verbal clues. For example, *first person:* "I worked as a medical secretary at this time" (sigh). *Second person:* "I worked as a medical secretary at	

this time and wasn't entirely happy with the set-up where I worked." After each role-play the person who was introduced is invited to comment on the assumptions.

25 mins

Closure
Sculptures

Members are asked to depict how they felt at the end of the group by imagining they are a sculpture and assuming a posture to show that. The group then form a circle, clasp hands and have a stretch.

5 mins

4 NON-VERBAL COMMUNICATION

AIMS
1 To encourage eye contact.
2 To increase awareness of others.
3 To become aware of our roles in relationships.
4 To promote touching between members.

MATERIALS Art paper, selection of art media.

ACTIVITY	METHOD	TIME
Introduction *Hobbies*	Members introduce themselves, then mime an interest or hobby for others to guess.	*10 mins*
Warm-up 1 *Wink games*	The leader divides the group into two circles, the inner one seated, with an extra chair which should remain empty. Members of the outer circle each stand behind a seat (the number of seats should equal the number of people standing). The person who is standing behind the empty chair tries to persuade one of those seated to move to their seat by winking at them. The others who are standing behind occupied seats can prevent this by touching the person in their chair when they try to move. Once the winker has managed to fill his seat, the person with the now empty chair continues.	*10 mins*
Main exercise *The silent dialogue*	Have members seated at a table or in a loose circle on the floor. Ask them to choose a partner and take one sheet of paper between them and the painting or drawing medium of their choice. They now have a non-verbal dialogue with their partner, using the paints, crayons and so on. After five minutes or so they change, find someone else in the room and start off a new conversation in the same manner, and so on until everyone has been with all other members of the group. During this activity the leader asks group members to think about such questions as: (a) Does this conversation feel relaxed, tense, amusing, aggressive? (b) Are there differences between partners, or is the pattern similar? (c) Are they aware of complementing their partner's dialogue or are they spoiling it? When this practical part of the exercise is complete, a discussion should follow on the above points.	*35–40 mins*

ACTIVITY	METHOD	TIME
Closure *Shoulder massage*	Standing in a circle, the group members turn so that they are facing the back of the person to their right. They then massage this person's shoulders for a few minutes. When the leader says change, everyone turns about so that they are now massaging the person who was initially doing it to them. While this is going on the leader encourages members to give feedback to their partners: do they like it; do they need to be more gentle or firm? Ask everyone to finish up with a quick pat on the back.	*5 mins*

4

5 NON-VERBAL COMMUNICATION

AIMS
1 To become more aware of our own non-verbal communication.
2 To encourage us to be aware of our feelings.
3 To promote trust in the group.
4 To increase our awareness of the way others see us.

MATERIALS Recorded music to induce relaxation and comfort, two garden canes per pair, paper and art materials.

ACTIVITY	METHOD	TIME
Introduction *Guess the feeling*	Members are seated on chairs in a circle. In turn they introduce themselves and then convey to the group, non-verbally, how they are feeling. The rest of the group try to guess what this is. Suggestions are then confirmed or denied by the person concerned.	*5 mins*
Warm-up *Wand dance*	The leader asks the group to form pairs; each pair takes two garden canes. The idea is for them to become joined by the canes by pressing their palms against the ends; they then have to move around the room to music without dropping them.	*5 mins*
Main exercise *Portraits*	Ask the group to make quick portraits of everyone else, for example 10 portraits in 20–25 mins, sign them and give them to the person concerned. The emphasis is that these should be a reflection of how you see this person rather than an accurate depiction of all their facial features. There can be some discussion on how members feel about receiving their portraits. Encourage members to take these with them when they leave the group.	*40 mins*
Closure *Rocking to music*	Two members are asked to sit on the floor with legs entwined to make themselves stable. Another member of the group sits in the space between their legs and the first two wrap their arms around them so that they are held securely. They then rock the person gently in time to music. This exercise is repeated, with each person having the opportunity to be the one who is rocked.	*10 mins*

4

EXPRESSING FEELINGS

Group Leader's Introduction

For various reasons many of us find it difficult to express our feelings directly and in this chapter our suggested activities facilitate this. By saying what we feel we help others understand us and this can lead to honest, open relationships with clear lines of communication.

We have a right to our own special feelings and denying them can lead to many complex problems, for ourselves and others. Showing our feelings helps to establish our own identity.

The workshops help us to deal with consequences of showing feelings, to explore this and to look at reasons for our often holding back. We are encouraged to support each other as we will often feel vulnerable when showing our true feelings.

● ACTIVITY LOCATOR

5

EXPRESSING FEELINGS

AIMS To highlight the fact that our feelings can affect our behaviour in different ways.

MATERIALS Pens, handout for main exercise.

ACTIVITY	METHOD	TIME
Introduction *Emotions*	Seated in a circle, members introduce themselves then do one or two rounds naming an emotion, such as joy, grief, frustration and so on.	*5 mins*
Warm-up *Choose an object*	Ask individuals to identify something in the room that could be used to describe how they are feeling at present. For example, "I feel like the clock, that time is running out for me."	*10 mins*
Main exercise *Expectations*	*Part 1* The leader gives each member the handout (page 71) for this exercise to complete. It may be useful for them to run through an example first of the type of thing required.	*15 mins*
	Part 2 Individuals are then invited to talk about each section on their form, sharing this information with others in the group.	*15 mins*
	Part 3 The leader facilitates discussion on the following points: (a) Do we need to feel the way we do to respond to others? (b) What right have we to our own special feelings? (c) How can our behaviour help the way we feel?	*15 mins*
Closure *Relaxation with focus*	The leader arranges the group in the suggested relaxation position on page 107 and uses the following text: 'First make yourself completely comfortable. If you are wearing glasses take them off and loosen any tight clothing at your neck and waist. Allow your body to sink into the floor. Let your legs and feet flop outwards. Enjoy the feeling of resting, of being completely supported. Let your eyes close.' *Pause …* 'Now become aware of your breathing. Follow the breath as it comes into and out of your body. Do not	

⑤

try to control it in any way — just observe the natural
rhythm of your breathing. As you breathe out,
imagine your whole body growing limp and heavy.
Each time you breathe out, imagine that you are
letting tension flow out of your body and mind. Focus
on the word 'peace' as the breath flows gently in and
out of your body.'

Pause ...
'I would now like you to think back over some of
the issues that were brought up over the course of
the workshop. Pick out something that you found
particularly useful for your situation. This may be
something that you came up with yourself or it
may have been a suggestion made by another
group member.'

Pause ...
'In a few moments you will open your eyes and will
take that useful image, phrase or suggestion with you
when you leave the room.'

10 mins

EXPRESSING FEELINGS

Choose a person in your life from one of the following categories, then complete the sections:

(a) Family member
(b) Boss or person in authority
(c) Friend
(d) Partner
(e) Child

What does this person expect from you?

How do these expectations make you feel?

Do they fit in with the expectations you have for yourself?

How do you feel as a result?

How do you then behave towards this person?

2 EXPRESSING FEELINGS

AIMS
1 To be able to give and receive compliments.
2 To increase awareness of situations and people influencing our feelings.
3 To develop self-esteem.

MATERIALS Ball/bean-bag, paper and pens, small container.

ACTIVITY	METHOD	TIME
Introduction Compliments	With the group seated in a circle, one member is asked by the leader to start by saying their name then throwing the ball to another in the group and paying them a compliment. This second person does the same and so on until everyone in the group has been mentioned.	5 mins
Warm-up Influences	Members do a round saying three things that make them angry, another saying what makes them happy and, finally, one saying what makes them sad. It may be easier to write these down initially.	20 mins
Main exercise Beliefs	Members write down three things that they believe in, such as life after death or equal rights for women. The pieces of paper are folded, collected by the group leader and put in a container and jumbled up. Each person takes a piece of paper and reads out the three beliefs. Others in the group then try and guess who wrote it, and why they arrived at their decision. The relevant individuals then admit ownership and expand on what their beliefs mean to them.	30 mins
Closure Something I have learned	Members take it in turns to say something that they have learned about themselves, followed by a round of revealing something they have learned about someone else in the group.	5 mins

5

3 EXPRESSING FEELINGS

AIMS
1 To practise expressing different emotions.
2 To promote insight into feelings.

MATERIALS
Collection of magazines and newspapers, scissors, prepared cards with a number of different moods written on them, selection of small cards of various colours, paper and pens.

ACTIVITY	METHOD	TIME
Introduction *Colour cards*	The leader arranges a variety of cards of different colours on the floor in the middle of the seated group. Members introduce themselves and choose a card which they feel reflects their present mood.	*5 mins*
Warm-up 1 *Mime an emotion*	The leader asks the group to break up into pairs. A person from each pair collects from the leader a card which has an emotion written on it. They then have to try and convey this feeling through mime to their partners. Once this has been guessed the other person in the pair collects a different card and does the same. This continues until each have had three or four attempts.	*10 mins*
Warm-up 2 *Limericks*	Staying in the same pairs, each couple come up with a limerick about one emotion, writing it down. Ensure that each pair chooses a different emotion. For example, "There was a young man from Bangor who suffered from bouts of anger"; "There was an old woman from Leith who was subject to terrible grief". When the limericks have been completed, pairs form a large group and take turns to recite them.	*10–15 mins*
Warm-up 3 *Group scream*	Group members hold hands, form a circle and crouch down. Starting with a soft murmur, they very slowly begin to stand up, raising their voices as they go until they reach screaming pitch when they are upright, still holding hands with arms in the air. Do this two or three times, then discuss how this felt.	*5 mins*
Main exercise *Associated feelings*	Present a collection of magazines and newspapers and have each member choose a picture of a person and cut this out. Now ask the following questions: (a) What emotions are evident in the picture?	

5

(b) What do you think has happened/is happening?

(c) Has there been a time when you felt the same way?

Now have them imagine that they are the person in the picture and to introduce themselves to their partner or the small group as that person, saying who they are, a little about their circumstances and how that feels.

40 mins

Closure
De-roling

Go around each person in the group and have them say in which ways they are different from the person in their picture.

5–10 mins

Recommendations
Depending on the size of the group and how well they know each other, it may be easier for participants to do the main exercise in pairs or groups of three.

4 EXPRESSING FEELINGS

AIMS
1 To facilitate expression of feelings.
2 To gain insight into the way we express feelings.
3 To work together.

MATERIALS Scissors, magazines, paper, crayons, felt-tips.

ACTIVITY	METHOD	TIME
Introduction *Difficult feelings*	Members are seated on chairs in a circle and are asked by the leader to introduce themselves by saying their name, sharing a feeling which they find difficult to express and saying why.	*5 mins*
Warm-up *Objects*	Each member is asked to take a piece of paper and drawing materials. The leader explains that they are to draw themselves as an object or a creature. If people appear to be having difficulties, make some suggestions — tree, animal, house and so on. After a few minutes each person is asked to describe the object to the rest of the group using the first person: for example, "I'm a cat, I like my home comforts and I'm independent." Members should be encouraged to say how they feel as this object or animal.	*20 mins*
Main exercise *Vignettes*	Members are asked to form pairs. Each pair is asked to look through magazines and to cut out a picture that depicts people communicating in some way. The leader asks them to have a good look at the picture (pairs look only at their own picture) and decide what the people may be communicating about, as they are going to be asked to enact this in front of the rest of the group, as if they were the people in the picture. The leader then collects the cut-out pictures and spreads them out in front of the group. As each pair enacts their 'vignette' the rest of the group has to choose the picture they are depicting. Discussion afterwards should include: clues that people picked up from the pictures; how others guessed which picture was being enacted; elements of themselves that came into the members' role-play; how they chose a picture; how they felt about acting out the scene.	*30 mins*
Closure *Free expression*	Members are asked to share with the group a feeling they would like to be able to express more freely and suggest how they might do this.	*5 mins*

EXPRESSING FEELINGS

AIMS
1 To facilitate expression of feelings.
2 To encourage physical ventilation of feelings.
3 To increase awareness of ways in which our feelings are influenced.

MATERIALS
Large sheet of paper to be pinned on the wall, a dozen 3" (8cm) square coloured cards in a variety of shades, crayons, felt-tips, spray-paints, A4 paper, pens, four different types of recorded music.

ACTIVITY	METHOD	TIME
Introduction *Uncomfortable feelings*	With members seated on chairs in a circle, each person introduces themselves and expresses a feeling they are uncomfortable with.	*5 mins*
Warm-up 1 *Crossings*	Members are asked to stand at one side of the room and to cross to the other side, depicting different emotions as they go. The leader shouts out some examples for the first few 'crossings' and then asks individuals to suggest some. Discuss afterwards how people felt.	*5 mins*
Warm-up 2 *Graffiti*	The leader pins a large sheet of paper on the wall and provides a variety of art materials. Members are then asked to express anything they like on this sheet of paper. All members are encouraged to stay up at the wall for a few minutes. After everyone has finished, the discussion can be started by asking people how they felt doing the graffiti: for example, have they ever defaced something or have they felt like it but been unable to do it? What were the reasons?	*15 mins*
Main exercise *Musical emotions*	Members are given a piece of paper and pen and asked to sit or lie in a comfortable position, perhaps using bean-bags. They are then told that different types of music will be played and that they are to write down any feelings they experience in response to each piece of music. Use four different types of music, and play each for two or three minutes. At the end of the music, members are asked to share their responses to each piece of music in turn. In discussion they say whether it was a comfortable or uncomfortable feeling, whether there were any associations that went with it, and so on. Ask how	

they express their feelings, given that writing
them down is not normal practice. Can they think
of ways of dealing with or expressing their
feelings differently?

30 mins

Closure
Colour cards

Cards in a wide variety of colours and shades are
spread on the floor in the middle of the group. Each
member is asked to choose a card that reflects the
way they feel at present. They are asked to say why
in a few words.

5 mins

ASSERTION TRAINING

Because we are brought up to look after other people and consider their needs, we are often out of touch with our own. Even if we know what our needs are we may feel we do not have the right to pursue them, particularly if they appear to conflict with the needs of others. We have to learn to value our own views and decisions and not let others force their will upon us.

Assertiveness is often confused with selfishness or aggression, with putting our own needs before other people's and pursuing them regardless of the effect on others. This is not assertiveness. Assertiveness is:

- recognizing our needs and asking openly and directly for what we want;
- recognizing and respecting the rights and needs of others;
- relating to people in personal and working situations in an open and honest way;
- feeling responsible for and in control of our own actions;
- not seeing situations in terms of win or lose, but being prepared to compromise;
- being able to resolve difficulties and disputes in a way that feels comfortable and just to those involved.

Becoming more assertive should allow us to challenge situations with more confidence. Saying no to people should become easier as we shed the guilty feelings this can sometimes bring. Assertion involves remaining calm and clear about what we want and having the strength and confidence to stand by this when we are up against opposition. For some of us this is not a simple task, but it does get easier with practice.

● ACTIVITY LOCATOR

6

1 ASSERTION TRAINING

AIMS
1 To facilitate ventilation of feelings.
2 To increase awareness of being assertive.
3 To promote insight into our behaviour.

MATERIALS None.

ACTIVITY	METHOD	TIME
Introduction *Names and rhythms*	Members are seated in a circle and the leader asks them to start by doing a round of their names. This is followed by a round of names with a rhythm attached to it, usually highlighting the syllables. When everyone has a rhythm, a few rounds are done, each one faster than the one before.	*5 mins*
Warm-up 1 *Yes/no*	Group members are asked to get into pairs. They then start a dialogue using only the words 'yes' and 'no', as follows: one partner sits, saying "yes", while the other stands above and facing, saying "no", in various tones of persuasion. After a short time they change positions. (Using a chair to stand on can sometimes add impact to this exercise.) The group leader then encourages participants to say how they felt during the exercise: which role felt most comfortable or uncomfortable; did it bear any relation to the way people usually behave? And so on.	*10 mins*
Warm-up 2 *When yes means no*	Seated in a circle, members are asked to recollect the last occasion they said "yes" when they really meant "no".	*10 mins*
Main exercise *Role-play*	Members pair up again and take it in turns to role-play the occasion they thought of in Warm-up 2, only this time saying "no". The rest of the group watch one pair at a time and help out if they are finding it difficult.	*30 mins*
Closure *Who I need to be more assertive with*	Group members return to the circle and take it in turns to name someone they need to be more assertive with and to say what they would most like to say to them.	*5 mins*

6

2 ASSERTION TRAINING

AIMS
1 To facilitate expression of feelings and ideas.
2 To promote assertiveness.
3 To promote self-esteem.

MATERIALS   Paper, pens.

ACTIVITY	METHOD	TIME
Introduction *Change the movement*	Members are seated in a circle and introduce themselves one by one. The leader explains that the introductory exercise involves everyone standing up and moving around the room. Then one person is asked to walk round in a different way, for example hopping, and everyone else must copy. Thereafter anyone can change the movement at any time and everyone then copies them.	*5 mins*
Warm-up 1 *I like …*	Group members are asked to mingle and when they meet someone to say something that they like: for example, "I like holidays in the sun"; "I like fillet steak." Carry this on until most people have met each other a couple of times.	*5–10 mins*
Warm-up 2 *Snippets*	Two members are asked to volunteer to have a conversation in the middle of the group. Two chairs are put in the middle. Another two members volunteer to write down a topic of conversation each on pieces of paper that will be handed to the members in the middle, who then have to start a conversation and try to bring it round to their 'topic'. Allow two or three minutes for this. The group then has to guess what the topics were and members say how they found the exercise. Repeat with two more volunteers.	*10–15 mins*
Main exercise *Weekend away*	The group is divided into smaller teams of four. Each person is asked to choose a type of holiday they would like to go on from the following: camping, outdoor pursuits, city break, island hopping, lazing in the sun, sightseeing, crafts. Encourage each person to choose a different type of holiday from the other three people in their team. Give instructions as follows: "You are all going on holiday together for a long weekend. In your team it is your task to try to explain why you want to go on your particular type of holiday and to give reasons	

6

why others should choose to come too."

After about 15 minutes, teams come back into a large group, where discussion of the exercise is facilitated by group leaders. Discussion points:

(a) Did people use compromising, negotiating and assertiveness skills?

(b) What was decided in each team?

(c) How was the decision made?

(d) Did people give in easily?

(e) Was anyone determined not to give in?

30 mins

Closure
*Something I have
learned*

Each person is asked to say something they have learned in the group.

5 mins

3 ASSERTION TRAINING

AIMS
1 To encourage identification of needs.
2 To facilitate expression of ideas and feelings.
3 To have fun.

MATERIALS   Paper, pens.

ACTIVITY	METHOD	TIME
Introduction *Story telling*	Members are seated on chairs in a circle and introduce themselves by saying their first names. The group leader then asks one member to start telling a story and each member in turn adds to the story, saying as much or as little as they want until the story is finished.	*10 mins*
Warm-up *Listen to me*	Members are asked to divide into pairs and to stand opposite one another. The group leader then asks members to try to out-talk each other. If one person gains the attention of the other and makes them start listening, then the latter loses. The leader then asks group members to mill around, trying to make the person they are passing listen to them but not listening themselves. Anyone who is made to listen puts their hand on the other's shoulder and follows them around silently. The game ends when there is one person walking around with everyone following silently, or when two people are still battling.	*10–15 mins*
Main exercise *Sharing a house*	The group leader asks half the group to do the 'work' in the main exercise and the other half are told they are going to observe. The 'workers' are then told that they will be sharing a house and the following information is given: (a) they are to negotiate the house 'rules' and agree how bills will be paid; (b) there is one less bedroom than there are members; (c) the rent is £600 a month; (d) there is a phone in the house which is not a pay phone; (e) electricity is paid quarterly and there is no meter; (f) there is one dining-room, one kitchen, one bathroom and one sitting-room.	

The observers are asked to make notes on points such as:

(a) who made decisions,
(b) how decisions were made/arrived at,
(c) who gave in to others' decisions.

The group then assembles and discusses observers' findings, how the other group felt and so on.

25–30 mins

Closure
Assertion needs

Each member is asked to tell the group one way in which they need to become more assertive.

5 mins

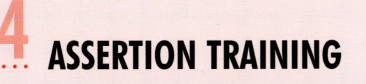

4 ASSERTION TRAINING

AIMS
1 To increase awareness of our assumptions.
2 To increase awareness of our reactions to people.
3 To promote discussion.
4 To have fun.

MATERIALS Flip-chart with pens.

ACTIVITY	METHOD	TIME
Introduction *My favourite meal*	Members are seated on chairs in a circle. They introduce themselves and tell the group what their favourite meal is.	*5 mins*
Warm-up *30 seconds*	A member of the group is asked to volunteer to talk on a subject for 30 seconds. (The leader can volunteer if no one wants to go first.) Topics may include cars, fashion, politics and so on. Someone in the group who has a watch with a second hand can offer to keep note of the time. When the first speaker has finished, they have to think of a topic for the person on their left to talk about for 30 seconds. The sequence continues until everyone has spoken on a topic. If someone has genuine difficulty in talking for 30 seconds, the leader should encourage them to talk just for as long as possible.	*5–10 mins*
Main exercise *Fact or fiction*	*Part 1* Members are asked to choose a partner and to discuss assumptions made about assertive people. For example, some people believe assertive women are unfeminine, assertive people only care about themselves, and so on. This should be discussed for about five minutes and then pairs are asked to come back to the large group and to share their thoughts. One member of the group can volunteer to write this on the flip-chart. Discuss. *Part 2* Members are then asked to go back into pairs and discuss different types of reactions to people as regards being assertive with, for example, authority figures, friends or salesmen. This goes on for five or ten minutes. Then everyone is asked to come back to the large group and each pair feeds back. Write findings on a flip-chart. Discussion points to	

6

consider: it may be more difficult to be assertive with people in authority or with family. Leaders facilitate discussion as to why it is easier with some people than with others.

30–40 mins

Closure
Relaxation with focus

The leader arranges the group in the relaxation position suggested on page 107 and uses the following text:
'First make yourself completely comfortable. If you are wearing glasses take them off and loosen any tight clothing at your neck and waist. Allow your body to sink into the floor. Let your legs and feet flop outwards. Enjoy the feeling of resting, of being completely supported. Let your eyes close.'

Pause ...
'Now become aware of your breathing. Follow the breath as it comes into and goes out of your body. Do not try to control it in any way — just observe the natural rhythm of your breathing. As you breathe out, imagine your whole body growing limp and heavy. Each time you breathe out, imagine that you are letting tension flow out of your body and mind. Focus on the word 'strength' as the breath flows gently in and out of your body.'

Pause ...
'In a few moments you will open your eyes and you will feel emotionally stronger. You will take that feeling with you when you leave the room.'

5 mins

5 ASSERTION TRAINING

AIMS
1 To clarify what assertion is.
2 To experience a variety of ways of dealing with situations.
3 To promote self-esteem.

MATERIALS Flip-chart and pen.

ACTIVITY	METHOD	TIME
Introduction *I'm good at …*	Each member is asked to introduce themselves and tell the group something they are good at.	*5 mins*
Warm-up and main exercise combined *Role-play*	The leader divides the group into groups of four and explains that each member will take a turn at playing the following roles: assertive, aggressive, passive, manipulative. The leader ensures that everyone is aware of the differences between these roles. This is effected by a 'brainstorm' using the flip-chart. (For the leader's reference, *Assertiveness* is described on page 81.) *Aggression* expresses feelings in a way that punishes, threatens or belittles the other person; it disregards the rights of others; a person who is aggressive aims to get their own way no matter what. *Passivity*, in the present context, means not standing up for our rights; allowing others to take advantage of us; avoiding responsibility for making choices; not being in control of our lives. If we are *Manipulative*, we are unable to ask directly for what we want, so we try to get what we want indirectly, by 'playing games' or trying to make others feel guilty. There are four situations for the leader to give to each group: (a) Four friends are trying to decide where to go for an evening out. (b) A family situation: mother wants the children to visit grandmother, who is ill in hospital; the children do not want to go. (c) Returning faulty goods: this involves a shopkeeper and three customers. (d) Three employees all want two days off at short notice and need the permission of their boss.	

6

The groups are asked to enact the situations, ensuring that each member gets a chance to take on all of the four roles described. At the end of the role-play there can be a brief discussion, facilitated by the leader, on members' reactions to the exercise. Questions might include:

(a) What roles felt comfortable?
(b) What roles felt uncomfortable?
(c) What roles were easy to play?
(d) What roles were difficult to play?

50 mins

Closure
Changes

Ask members to relate this experience to their own degree of assertiveness in other situations.

Members are asked to think of one thing they could change to help them become more assertive and to share this with the rest of the group.

5 mins

6 ASSERTION TRAINING

AIMS **1** To explore fears of being assertive.
2 To promote change.
3 To facilitate sharing and support in the group.

MATERIALS Bean-bag, paper, flip-chart and pens.

ACTIVITY	METHOD	TIME
Introduction *Saying no*	With members seated in a circle, each person is asked in turn by the leader to introduce themselves and tell the group of one occasion when they were not able to say no or a time when they wanted to say no but were unable to do so.	*5–10 mins*
Warm-up *Excuses*	With the group still seated in a circle, the bean-bag is thrown to someone who then has to give an example of an excuse they might use instead of saying no: for example, "I'm washing my hair tonight"; "I've got to visit my grandmother." Keep this going until everyone has had a chance. Follow this by asking members to do a round of what they really want to say.	*10 mins*
Main exercise *Effects of saying no*	Each member is given a piece of paper on which they write their fears about saying no and how that makes them feel. The papers are folded and given to the group leader who then hands them out again to members. Each person then reads out what is on their paper and someone writes the fears or concerns on the flip-chart. The leader facilitates discussion on challenging these fears and what can be done about them, thus altering the effect of saying no.	*30 mins*
Closure *What I'm taking away*	Members are asked to write down something that they are taking away from the group that they will try out in the coming week. They are then asked to tell the group what this is.	*5–10 mins*

6

DECISION MAKING

Group Leader's Introduction

Decisions must be taken in everyday life and an inability in this regard can hold us back in many ways. To gain control of our lives we have to learn to take responsibility for making our own decisions. Allowing other people to make them for us can lead to resentment for one or both parties, frustration, unmet needs and feelings of impotence.

Some decision making may be seen as a matter of a practical problem solving, but other instances may involve the emotions, acknowledging our feelings and needs at times, and trusting in our intuition.

Making decisions may have effects on other people's lives and in the workshops we encourage people to explore the motives and influences that affect us: for example, do we primarily meet our own needs or do we sacrifice these for others? At times we may look back on past decisions in a negative way, feeling that the path we took was not perhaps the right one. Such reflections are not fruitful, since the past cannot be changed. The emphasis should be on seeing them as a learning experience which can be used to help with future difficulties.

● ACTIVITY LOCATOR

7

DECISION MAKING

AIMS
1. To explore the decision-making process.
2. To discuss the effects of making a decision.
3. To promote understanding of the decision-making process.

MATERIALS   Flip-chart, pens.

ACTIVITY	METHOD	TIME
Introduction *Significant decisions*	Members are seated on chairs in a circle. Each person is asked by one of the group leaders to share a decision they have made in their life which had particular significance for them.	*5 mins*
Warm-up *Easy and difficult*	Leaders ask members to get into pairs. Each pair is then asked to discuss decision making in the following way: (a) decisions they find easy to make, (b) decisions they find difficult to make. Encourage members to think about why there are differences. The pairs are then asked to come back into a large circle and a volunteer writes on the flip-chart. The chart is divided into two columns headed EASY DECISIONS and DIFFICULT DECISIONS and members are asked in turn to say what they came up with in their pairs. This is written onto the flip-chart.	*10–15 mins*
Main exercise *Why are decisions difficult?*	Using information on the flip-chart, the leaders encourage discussion of the question as to why some decisions are easy to make and some are difficult. They encourage members to voice their feelings about the significant decision they shared in the introduction: was this an easy or a difficult decision to make, and why? The leaders guide the discussion so that it covers the following points: (a) Did the influence of others affect the decision-making process? (b) Did the outcome affect others? (c) What were the consequences of the outcome for the individual? (d) What changes occurred as a result of the process?	*30 mins*
Closure *If I knew then what I know now*	Ask people to think again about their significant decision and to share it with the group once more. If they were in that position now, would they make the same decision?	*10 mins*

⑦

2 DECISION MAKING

AIMS
1 To promote decision making.
2 To examine our role in the decision-making process.
3 To have some fun.
4 To promote self-confidence.

MATERIALS None.

ACTIVITY	METHOD	TIME
Introduction *A good decision*	Everyone is seated on chairs in a circle. Members are asked to introduce themselves and to tell the group about a decision they have made that week that they feel pleased with.	*5–10 mins*
Warm-up *Orchestra*	The group is to imagine itself as an orchestra. One person goes out of the room and from the remainder of the group a 'leader' is chosen. This person has to mime playing a variety of musical instruments which the others will imitate, trying to change instruments simultaneously with the leader. The member who is outside returns and has to try and guess who the leader is. This should be repeated several times.	*10 mins*
Main exercise *Ward round*	The leader explains to members that this exercise involves enacting a ward round or multidisciplinary team meeting. It will require two 'patients' and various team members. The team members will discuss the management and treatment of patients. The team members involved could include consultant psychiatrist, charge nurse, staff nurse, student nurse, registrar, medical student, occupational therapist, social worker, clinical psychologist and so on — enough to ensure that each member of the group has a role. Ask each member to choose a role. The two 'patients' can then decide what their reasons for being in hospital are and tell the team briefly some of their difficulties and how they are progressing in hospital. (If preferred, group leaders can write out a short synopsis for the two 'patients', with a brief history of presenting problems, how long the patients have been in hospital and progress to date.) Then ask the two patients to sit at one end of the room and the team to gather at the other end and form a meeting. Let them decide who is going to	

⑦

99

co-ordinate the meeting and what its format will be.
When they have decided that, they can begin to
discuss patient number one and their management
and treatment. They should be encouraged to see and
interview the patient and convey decisions
to them. The process is repeated with patient
number two.

When this is finished, leaders should facilitate
discussion of the exercise and how it went:
How did people feel in the different roles?
Who made decisions?
Who left decision making to others?
Who was passive?
Was anyone aggressive?
How were decisions made?

40 mins

Closure
De-roling

The leader asks each person in turn to state the ways
in which they are different from the character they
played in the role-play.

5 mins

⑦

3 DECISION MAKING

AIMS
1 To receive feedback from others about how they see us.
2 To increase awareness of the way we make decisions.
3 To improve self-esteem.
4 To facilitate feelings of 'being in control of our lives'.

MATERIALS   Pens and scrap paper, art paper and a selection of art media.

ACTIVITY	METHOD	TIME
Introduction *Landmarks*	Members introduce themselves by stating their names and giving a brief personal history. This is done in the style of a 'life walk'; that is, taking a big step forward for every significant event or landmark in their lives. Some people may only take a few steps; others may walk the length of the room. Examples of landmarks/events may be: nursery school, exams, births/deaths, marriage/divorce and so on.	*10–15 mins*
Warm-up *Ego sandwich*	Have members in chairs seated in a circle. One person volunteers to turn their chair outwards so they are positioned with their back to the rest of the group. The others are then encouraged to: (a) say a few things they like about this person; followed by (b) a few things they would like them to change; and finally (c) things they like about them once again. Repeat this process with each person. The leader then encourages some discussion of how the exercise felt for the participants. The warm-up is concluded by having each person decide what they would like to change most about themselves, and why.	*20–25 mins*
Main exercise *Maps*	Give the group a few minutes to think about an important decision they made in their lives and to write down the brief outlines of this. Next, taking art paper and materials, individuals depict this decision in the form of a life map or journey: What was happening in their lives at the time? What options were open to them? What forces were influencing the decision? What has this decision led to?	

⑦

In the large group, members are invited to talk about their pictures. If members are reflecting on the decision in a negative way, leaders should emphasize that the value of the exercise is in looking at what can be learned from each situation to help with future decision making.

35 mins

Closure
Relaxation with focus

Have the group arranged in the relaxation position suggested on page 107 and use the following text: 'First make yourself completely comfortable. If you are wearing glasses take them off and loosen any tight clothing at your neck and waist. Allow your body to sink into the floor. Let your legs and feet flop outwards. Enjoy the feeling of resting, of being completely supported. Let your eyes close.'

Pause ...
'Now become aware of your breathing. Follow the breath as it comes into and leaves your body. Do not try to control it in any way — just observe the natural rhythm of your breathing. As you breathe out, imagine that you are letting tension flow out of your body and mind. Focus on the word 'strength' as the breath flows gently in and out of your body.'

Pause ...
'Now that your body is relaxed I would like your to conjure up a mental image of your illustrated journey.'

Pause ...
'Place yourself in this scene so that you are standing with this landscape behind you.'

Pause ...
'Now imagine that you are very slowly walking away from this scene, which is beginning to fade from view. Be aware of how strong you feel leaving this behind. In a few moments you will open your eyes and you will feel emotionally stronger. You will take this feeling with you when you leave the room.'

5 mins

4 DECISION MAKING

AIMS
1. To explore how decisions are made.
2. To promote decision making.
3. To have fun.

MATERIALS Paper, pens, one extra chair, a bottle of paint, a variety of objects of interesting shapes, textures and colours — enough for the number of members.

ACTIVITY	METHOD	TIME
Introduction Characteristics	With the group seated on chairs in a circle, everyone introduces themselves and names two characteristics they possess. The leader asks them to consider, if they could keep only one characteristic, what choice they would make, and why.	10 mins
Warm-up Miming	A chair is placed in the middle of the circle. Members are invited to go into the middle and mime a use for the chair (as a pram, boat and so on) and the others are encouraged to guess what it is. This can be repeated by using other objects, such as a paint bottle, a bath scrubber or a baby's bottle.	5–10 mins
Main exercise Plane crash	The leader gives each person a small piece of paper and a pen. Members are then asked to think of an object and to write it on the piece of paper. It should be the first object that comes to mind. Members then form groups of five. The leader tells them that they, as a group, have been involved in a plane crash: one of them has a broken leg and cannot walk, but the others have only minor injuries. The crash has occurred in a jungle. Their task is to get out of the jungle, having to make a pathway through the trees, fight off wild animals and cross a river. They have the five listed objects to help them. Each group writes down how they are going to escape. Then ask everyone to come back to form a large group. Each set, in turn, presents their solution, saying what their objects were and how they planned their escape. The leader facilitates a discussion of the ways the decisions were made in the group, asking the following questions: (a) Who made the most suggestions? (b) Who disagreed?	

⑦

(c) Who agreed?

(d) Did anyone not make any suggestions?

(e) Who compromised?

(f) What was the decision-making process like?

(g) How did individuals feel about their role in the group?

(h) Is this a reflection of their behaviour outside the group?

40 mins

Closure
Recall

With the group seated in a circle and a number of objects of interesting shapes, textures and colours placed on the floor in the centre, members are asked to take an object of their choice. They are to study the object, paying particular attention to the scent, shape, colour, contours and so on. After a few minutes the objects are replaced in the centre and the members are asked to close their eyes and visualize their object, recalling all its characteristics. After allowing enough time for this, the leader asks the group to open their eyes and pick out their objects again to see if they have remembered correctly.

10–15 mins

5 DECISION MAKING

AIMS
1 To promote decision making.
2 To increase self-esteem.
3 To promote insight into oneself and others.

MATERIALS A4 paper and pens for each member; large sheet of drawing paper for each member; drawing materials.

ACTIVITY	METHOD	TIME
Introduction *My grandmother went to market*	Members are seated in a circle. After they have introduced themselves there is a game of 'My grandmother went to market': the first person starts off by saying "My grandmother went to market and bought a loaf of bread." The second person repeats this and adds another item. This carries on round the group. Anyone who forgets an item is out of the game, which carries on until only one person is left or until it has gone on long enough if there are a few people persevering.	*5 mins*
Warm-up 1 *Colours*	Members mill around the room. The leader or a volunteer member shouts out a colour and people then have to look around the room and find something of that colour and touch it. Repeat about ten times.	*5 mins*
Warm-up 2 *Exchange*	Each person is asked to say which characteristic in themselves they would like to give up and exchange for another one, and why.	*10 mins*
Main exercise *Three plus two qualities*	Each member is given a piece of paper and a pen. The paper is torn into five strips. Members write down on three separate strips three positive qualities they feel they have (generous, considerate, hard-working and so on). If people have difficulty in thinking of three, they should write down two or at least one. Once everyone has finished, the group can be divided into groups of four or five. Each person takes it in turn to read out their qualities and then the rest of the group decide on two more qualities for each person. These are written down on the other two strips of paper, but only if the person agrees that they are true. When everyone has had their turn, ask them to return to a large circle. Each person is asked to choose the quality that means the most to them	

and to say whether it was a quality they were given or wrote themselves. If there is time, encourage a general discussion on how people found the exercise and how and why they decided on the one most important quality.

30 mins

Closure
Presents

Each person is given a large piece of drawing paper on which they put their name, either at the top or in a corner. Everyone then mills around and can either write or draw on each person's paper — to give them a present. Papers are left on the floor and people move from one to another. When everyone has finished, members are invited to discuss what they received. If there are any questions in their minds they can ask why they have been given a particular item, and so on.

10–15 mins

GROUP POSITION FOR RELAXATION CLOSURES

In the lying position the group are linked by heads or hands touching. In the sitting position they are linked by touching shoulders with neighbours.

BIBLIOGRAPHY

Bond T, *Games for Social and Life Skills*, Hutchinson, London, 1986.

Brandes S & Phillips H, *Gamesters' Handbook*, Stanley Thornes, London, 1977.

Brandes S & Phillips H, *Gamesters' Handbook 2*, Stanley Thornes, London, 1982.

Dynes R, *Creative Games in Groupwork*, Winslow Press/Speechmark Publishing, Bicester, 1990.

Jennings S, *Creative Drama in Groupwork*, Winslow Press/Speechmark Publishing, Bicester, 1986.

Liebmann M, *Art Therapy for Groups*, Croom Helm, London, 1986.

Remocker AJ & Storch ET, *Action Speaks Louder*, Churchill Livingstone, London, 1977.

Yalom ID, *The Theory and Practice of Group Psychotherapy*, Basic Books, New York, 1983.